GET TWO-GETHER BOOKS

Celebrate Family

Heidi Bratton

CPH
SAINT LOUIS

Love the LORD your God with all your heart and with all your soul and with all your strength. These commandments that I give you today are to be upon your hearts. Impress them on your children. Talk about them when you sit at home and when you walk along the road, when you lie down and when you get up. Deuteronomy 6:5–7

God has placed you in a very special family. Families love and take care of each other. Families teach about God's love in what they say and in what they do to show God's love through Jesus. How blessed we are to celebrate our own very special family!

C is for ceremony.

E is for embrace.

L and E

are for loving elders.

B is for babies.

R is for relaxing.

A is for acceptance.

A b C + 6
1 2 3
- +

T
is for teaching.

A
+
+
+
+
+
6
+
+
+
+
+
1

E

is for eating.

F is for friends.

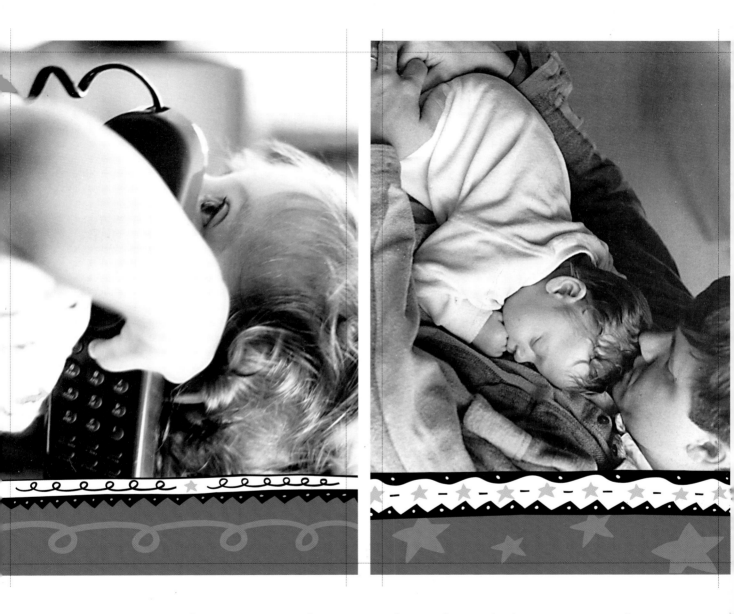

Clip these Get "Two-Gether" postcards and send them to loved ones.
Use the postcards to share the good news of God's love.

PostCard

Photograph by: Heidi Bratton © 2000 Get Two-Gether: Celebrate Family CPH

PostCard

Photograph by: Heidi Bratton © 2000 Get Two-Gether: Celebrate Family CPH

A

is for animals.

M

is for memories.

I, L, and Y

are for I love you ...

and God does

too!

For my Grama Egan,
who remembers every baptism, birthday,
anniversary, and Christmas,
and has spent her entire life
dedicated to celebrating family.
Thank you, Grama.
I love you.

Scripture quotations taken from the HOLY BIBLE, NEW INTERNATIONAL VERSION®. NIV®.
Copyright © 1973, 1978, 1984 by International Bible Society.
Used by permission of Zondervan Publishing House. All rights reserved.

Copyright © 2000 Heidi Bratton
Published by Concordia Publishing House
3558 S. Jefferson Avenue, St. Louis, MO 63118-3968
Manufactured in the United States of America

Cover and interior design by Karol Bergdolt

1   2   3   4   5   6   7   8   9   10   09   08   07   06   05   04   03   02   01   00

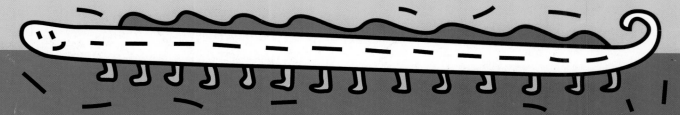